Conquering all the Tartarus bosses in Hades 2

Your Definitive Guide to Boss Fights, Strategies, and Advanced Combat Tactics in the Underworld

Henry D. Grim

Gratitude

To all the readers and buyers of "Conquering all the Tartarus bosses in Hades 2," we extend our heartfelt gratitude. Your support and enthusiasm for our book have been truly inspiring, and we are honored to have shared the wonders of Hades with you.

We would like to express our deepest thanks to each and every one of you for setting out on this journey with us. Your curiosity, passion, and love for adventure have made this experience unforgettable, and we are grateful for the opportunity to be a part of your Hades adventure.

Special thanks to our family, friends, and loved ones for their unwavering support and encouragement throughout this endeavor. Your belief in us has been a source of strength and inspiration, and we are forever grateful for your love and support.

To all our readers and buyers, thank you for joining us on this adventure. We hope that "Conquering all the Tartarus bosses in Hades 2" has brought you joy, excitement, and a sense of wonder, and we look forward to sharing many more adventures with you in the future.

With deepest gratitude,
Henry D. Grim

Copyright © 2024 by Henry D. Grim

All rights reserved.

No part of this publication may be reproduced, distributed, or transmitted in any form or by any means, including photocopying, recording, or other electronic or mechanical methods, without the prior written permission of the publisher, except in the case of brief quotations embodied in critical reviews and certain other noncommercial uses permitted by copyright law.

TABLE OF CONTENTS

INTRODUCTION 7
OVERVIEW OF THE GAME 7
    Purpose of the Guide 9

CHAPTER 1 13
BOSS FIGHT BASICS 13
    Preparing for Battles 15

CHAPTER 3 19
FACING HECATE: THE HEADMISTRESS 19
    Hecate's Move List and Descriptions 20
    Crossed Flames 20

CHAPTER 3 25
STRATEGIES FOR DEFEATING HECATE 25
    General Boss Fight Strategy 25
    Phase Breakdown 26
    Specific Moves Handling 28

CHAPTER 4 32
CONFRONTING SCYLLA AND THE SIRENS 32
    Introduction to the Trio 32
    Scylla and the Sirens' Attack List 32
    Bubble Projectile Attack 35
    Strategy to Overcome the Trio 37

CHAPTER 5 39
BATTLE STRATEGY FOR SCYLLA AND THE SIRENS 39
    Focusing on Individual Band Members 39

CHAPTER 6 .... **47**

    BATTLING ERIS: GUARDIAN OF THE RIFT 47
        Introduction to Eris *47*
        Eris's Move List and Descriptions *47*
        Strategies for Battling Eris *51*

CHAPTER 7 .... **53**

    STRATEGY TO DEFEAT ERIS 53
        Best Load out Against Eris *53*

CHAPTER 8 .... **60**

    ADVANCED COMBAT TACTICS 60
        Maximizing Damage Output *60*
        Exploiting Boss Weaknesses *63*

CHAPTER 9 .... **66**

    EXPLORING FURTHER CHALLENGES 66

CONCLUSION **73**

INTRODUCTION

Overview of the Game

Welcome to Hades 2, the highly anticipated sequel to the critically acclaimed Hades. This game penetrates further into the mythic underworld, providing a unique and thrilling experience complete with violent combat, compelling plot, and complex gaming mechanics.

In Hades 2, you step into the shoes of Melinoë, the daughter of Persephone and sister to Zagreus, the protagonist of the first game. Melinoë's journey is set against the backdrop of Greek mythology, where she must navigate the treacherous realms of the underworld to confront her ultimate foe, Chronos, the god of time. Along the way, she encounters formidable enemies, Detailed challenges, and powerful allies who aid her in her quest.

The game builds upon the solid foundation laid by its predecessor, introducing new weapons, abilities, and a host of new characters from Greek mythology. The roguelike structure remains intact, meaning each run through the underworld is unique, with randomized levels and challenges that ensure no two playthroughs are the same. This keeps the gameplay fresh and engaging, encouraging players to adapt their strategies and make the most of each run.

The visual design of Hades 2 is stunning, with vibrant, hand-drawn art that brings the underworld to life. Each character is meticulously crafted, showcasing the developers' attention to detail and love for Greek mythology. The soundtrack, composed by Darren Korb, perfectly complements the game's atmosphere, providing an immersive audio experience that enhances the overall gameplay.

As you travel through Hades 2, you'll discover a fascinating story full of interesting characters and plot twists. The conversation is snappy and amusing, bringing dimension to the plot and making each encounter stand out. The game's storytelling is tightly intertwined with its gameplay, ensuring that every choice you make has a significant impact on the tale.

Overall, Hades 2 is a masterful blend of action, strategy, and storytelling, offering a gaming experience that is both challenging and rewarding. Whether you're a fan of the first game or new to the series, Hades 2 promises an epic adventure that will keep you hooked from start to finish.

Purpose of the Guide

This guide is designed to help you access the many challenges and complexities of Hades 2. Whether you are an expert of the underworld or a beginner to the series, this book will give you essential insights, methods, and ideas to improve your gameplay experience.

One of the primary goals of this guide is to familiarize you with the game's mechanics and features. Hades 2 introduces several new elements that may seem overwhelming at first, but with a little guidance, you'll quickly become adept at using them to your advantage. From understanding the various weapons and abilities to mastering the art of dodging and attacking, this guide covers all the essential aspects of combat and gameplay.

Additionally, this guide provides detailed strategies for overcoming the game's toughest bosses. Hades 2 is known for its challenging boss battles, each requiring a unique approach and strategy. By breaking down each boss's moves and patterns, this guide will help you develop effective tactics to defeat them and progress further in the game.

Exploration is another key aspect of Hades 2, and this guide will help you make the most of it. The underworld is filled with hidden secrets, powerful artifacts, and valuable resources that can aid you in your journey. This guide offers tips on how to find and utilize these items, ensuring that you are always well-equipped for the challenges ahead.

Along with fighting and exploration, this guide discusses the game's narrative and character relationships. Hades 2 presents a deep and intriguing story, with each character providing unique insights and tasks. This book gives an overview of the main plot and side tasks, allowing you to fully immerse yourself in the game's universe and discover all of its mysteries.

Ultimately, the purpose of this guide is to enhance your enjoyment of Hades 2. By providing clear and concise information, it aims to make your journey through the underworld as smooth and enjoyable as possible. Whether you're looking for combat tips, exploration strategies, or narrative insights, this guide has you covered.

With the knowledge and tactics presented in this guide, you may confidently go on your expedition. The underworld may be a dangerous place, but with proper planning and strategies, you may overcome its trials and emerge victorious. Enjoy your voyage to Hades 2, and may the gods guide you!

CHAPTER 1

Boss Fight Basics

Understanding Boss Mechanics

Boss fights in Hades 2 are intense, thrilling encounters that test your skills, strategy, and patience. To emerge victorious, it's crucial to understand the mechanics that govern these formidable opponents. Each boss has unique patterns, moves, and phases that you need to decipher and adapt to. Here's a closer look at how to break down these mechanics and use them to your advantage.

First and foremost, observe the boss's behavior. Each boss in Hades 2 has a set of attacks and patterns that they cycle through. These moves are often telegraphed by specific animations or sounds.

For example, Hecate, one of the early bosses, spins on herself before launching her Crossed Flames attack. By paying attention to these cues, you can anticipate the attack and position yourself accordingly.

Understanding the phases of a boss fight is also critical. Most bosses change their tactics as their health depletes, introducing new attacks or increasing the frequency of existing ones. For instance, Hecate adds the Sheep Curse attack when her health drops below 50%, making her more dangerous. Recognizing these phases helps you prepare and adjust your strategy mid-fight, ensuring you're always a step ahead.

Dodging and positioning are key components of surviving boss fights. Each boss's attacks have specific areas of effect, and knowing where to move can mean the difference between life and death. For example, when facing Hecate's Fiery Arc, dodging to the sides is more effective than backpedaling, giving you a chance to close in for a counterattack.

Another important aspect is understanding your environment. Boss arenas in Hades 2 are often littered with obstacles or interactive elements that can either help or hinder you. Use these to your advantage. For example, if there are pillars or walls, use them to block projectiles or hide from attacks while you plan your next move.

Finally, patience and practice are essential. Boss mechanics can seem overwhelming at first, but with each attempt, you'll become more familiar with their patterns and how to counter them. Take your time to learn and don't rush. Every defeat brings you closer to mastering the fight.

Preparing for Battles

Preparation is the cornerstone of success in Hades 2's boss battles. Going into a fight unprepared is a surefire way to end up back at the start. Here are some tips to ensure you're ready for whatever the underworld throws at you.

Firstly, make sure you have the right weapons and abilities. Each weapon in Hades 2 offers a different playstyle, and some are better suited for certain bosses. Experiment with different weapons to find one that complements your approach. For example, the Sister Blades provide rapid, nimble strikes ideal for evading and weaving through enemy attacks, but the Argent Skull enables strong ranged assaults. Additionally, equipping abilities that increase your damage or survivability can make a big difference. Look for boons that boost your attack power, health regeneration, or offer more dashes.

Boons from the gods are another crucial element of preparation. Each god offers unique enhancements that can turn the tide of battle in your favor. For instance, Apollo's boons might grant you extra damage on backstabs, while Hermes could provide you with increased speed and evasion. Choose boons that complement your playstyle and weapon choice. A balanced mix of offensive and defensive boons often works best, giving you the tools to both deal damage and survive the boss's onslaught.

Health and resources are also vital. Before entering a boss fight, ensure you're in full health and have any consumables you might need. Collect health upgrades and restorative items as you progress through the levels. If you find yourself low on health, consider taking a break from advancing to explore side paths that might contain health pickups or items that can help in the upcoming battle.

Learning from your previous encounters is another form of preparation. Each time you face a boss, take note of what worked and what didn't. Did you struggle with a particular attack? Did you run out of health too quickly? Use this information to refine your strategy. Maybe you need to focus more on dodging or perhaps switch to a different weapon or boon combination.

Finally, mental preparation is just as important as physical readiness. Boss fights in Hades 2 can be intense and stressful. Take a moment to compose yourself before entering the arena. Stay calm and focused during the fight. Panicking can lead to mistakes, so maintain a clear head and stick to your strategy.

CHAPTER 2

Facing Hecate: The Headmistress

Introduction to the Boss

In Hades 2, your path through the Underworld brings you face to face with Hecate, the Headmistress. She is not just any boss; she is a formidable witch and mentor turned adversary, barring your escape from Erebus. Hecate is a true test of skill, serving as the first major boss Melinoë must conquer. Her challenging attacks and devious strategies will push you to your limits, but understanding her move set and how to counter each attack can turn the tide in your favor. The following lesson will help you negotiate the complexities of confronting Hecate and emerge triumphant in this vital struggle.

Hecate's Move List and Descriptions

Hecate's arsenal of attacks can seem overwhelming at first, but with careful observation and strategic planning, you can master her patterns and defeat her. Here's a detailed look at each of her moves and how to handle them.

Crossed Flames

One of Hecate's primary attacks is Crossed Flames. She releases a slow-moving purple ring that expands outward in all directions before retracting back to her position. The attack is well-telegraphed as Hecate spins rapidly before launching the ring. To avoid damage, move away from the circle's path or dodge into the circle, get a few hits in, and then dodge out as it retracts. This move requires precise timing and spatial awareness, so practice your dodges to master this maneuver.

Fiery Arc

Hecate fires one or two curved arcs of flames directly at Melinoë. Occasionally, she follows up with an additional flame arc. This attack is signaled by a distinctive grunt from Hecate before the arcs appear. The key to evading Fiery Arc is to dodge to the left or right, sidestepping the flames. Once you've dodged, sprint in to damage Hecate or fire off a barrage of Special attacks from a safe distance.

Triple Divide Summon

In this move, Hecate summons two mirror clones of herself, creating a trio that emits green flames, rings, or orbs toward Melinoë. The move is indicated by Hecate vanishing into smoke before re-emerging with her clones. The best strategy here is to dart to the edge of the arena, dodging the projectiles while staying out of range of the flames or orbs. Focus on avoiding damage rather than immediately identifying the real Hecate among the clones.

Minion Summon

This attack is similar to the Sigil Ring attack but includes summoning several shades that throw projectiles at you. Hecate spins and generates a growing and retracting ring while surrounded by a translucent blue unbreakable shield. To counter this move, circle the arena, eliminating the summoned shades while keeping an eye on Hecate's rings and the orbs thrown by the minions. Clear the minions quickly to minimize the threat.

Sheep Curse

The Sheep Curse is a particularly tricky move where Hecate sends out an orb that, if it hits, transforms Melinoë into a slow-moving sheep for a short time. This curse typically happens when Hecate's health is below 50%. She brings up an unbreakable shield and then emits the cursed orb. Stay mobile and use your dodge ability to avoid the orb and any sigils or projectiles that may spawn during this phase. The curse lasts for about 10 seconds, so remain vigilant until you revert to normal.

Sigil Circles

Hecate spawns several fixed AoE (Area of Effect) sigil circles on the ground that cause damage after a short countdown. She cocoons up with an unbreakable shield before launching this move, although the telegraphing is similar to her other attacks. The best way to handle Sigil Circles is to dash out of the magic circles as soon as they spawn. Repeat this process until the move ends, ensuring you're always one step ahead of the damage zones.

Retracting Fiery Arcs

When Hecate's health drops below 50%, she introduces the Retracting Fiery Arcs. She releases three waves of green flames in different directions that eventually change course and return to her. This move is signaled by a distinctive grunt. To avoid the arcs, create as much distance from Hecate as possible and wait for the flames to retract. Once the arcs are gone, take the opportunity to unleash several Special attacks on her.

Facing Hecate is a test of endurance and adaptability. By understanding her moves and learning how to counter them, you can reduce the damage taken and find openings to attack. Remember, each loss is a lesson that brings you closer to victory. Stay focused, refine your strategy with each attempt, and soon, the Headmistress will be just another conquered foe on your journey through the underworld.

CHAPTER 3

Strategies for Defeating Hecate

General Boss Fight Strategy

Defeating Hecate in Hades 2 requires a blend of agility, patience, and keen observation. As the first significant boss Melinoë faces, Hecate's battle is designed to test your understanding of the game's mechanics and your ability to adapt to her varied attacks. The key to overcoming Hecate is mastering the art of dodging and finding the right moments to strike. Here are some overarching strategies to help you prevail.

Firstly, always stay mobile. Hecate's attacks, though powerful, are predictable once you understand their patterns. Constant movement will help you avoid her projectiles and AoE (Area of Effect) attacks. Utilize the arena's ample space to keep a safe distance whenever she launches an assault.

Dodging is your best friend; practice using it to evade her most dangerous moves.

Next, focus on long-range attacks. Melinoë's Special attacks are particularly useful in this fight. While Hecate is recovering from one of her moves or is momentarily immobile, use this opportunity to chip away at her health from a distance. This strategy minimizes the risk of getting hit while ensuring you continuously deal damage.

Lastly, patience is crucial. Rushing in for quick kills will likely result in more damage taken. Instead, adopt a methodical approach. Wait for clear openings in her defenses before going on the offensive. Learning her attack patterns will significantly reduce the damage you take, allowing you to outlast her in this grueling encounter.

Phase Breakdown
Hecate's battle can be divided into three distinct phases, each determined by her health bar.

Understanding the nuances of each phase will help you tailor your strategy as the fight progresses.

Phase 1: Above 66% Health

In the first phase, Hecate's attacks are less frequent and less complex. She primarily uses Crossed Flames and Fiery Arc. During this phase, focus on learning the timing and patterns of these attacks. Stay at a distance to avoid her initial onslaught and use ranged attacks to whittle down her health. The objective here is to minimize damage and conserve your resources for the more challenging phases ahead.

Phase 2: Between 66% and 33% Health

Once Hecate's health drops below 66%, she begins to mix in more complex moves like Triple Divide Summon and Minion Summon. These attacks increase the number of projectiles you need to dodge and introduce additional enemies to the battlefield. During this phase, it's vital to maintain mobility and prioritize the elimination of summoned minions to reduce the number of threats. Keep dodging and use the openings created by her recovery times to continue your assault.

Phase 3: Below 33% Health

The final phase starts when Hecate's health falls below 33%. Here, she ramps up the frequency and intensity of her attacks, including the dreaded Sheep Curse and Sigil Circles. The arena becomes more chaotic with a higher density of projectiles and damaging zones. Stay vigilant and keep your distance to avoid the Sheep Curse, as being transformed significantly hampers your mobility. Focus on survival by dodging meticulously and only attacking when you have a clear, safe opening. The key is to stay calm and methodically finish her off despite the increased pressure.

Specific Moves Handling

Hecate's arsenal is varied, but each move has telltale signs and effective counters. Let's break down how to handle her most challenging attacks.

Crossed Flames

This attack involves a purple ring expanding outwards and then retracting. To counter, move away from the expanding ring and dodge back inside as it retracts, allowing you to get in a few hits.

Fiery Arc

Hecate fires arcs of flames towards you. Dodge to the side to avoid the flames and then close in for attacks during her recovery.

Triple Divide Summon

Hecate summons two clones, creating a trio that attacks simultaneously. Focus on dodging their projectiles by staying on the move and at the arena's edge. Avoid the urge to attack immediately; instead, prioritize avoiding damage.

Minion Summon

She summons shades that hurl projectiles. Circle the arena, eliminating the minions quickly while keeping an eye on Hecate's position. Use ranged attacks to deal with minions without getting too close to her.

Sheep Curse

This move sends out an orb that can transform you into a sheep. Stay mobile and use your dodge ability to avoid it. If hit, focus on avoiding further damage until the curse wears off.

Sigil Circles

Hecate spawns damaging sigils on the ground. Watch for the sigils to appear and dash out of their range immediately. Repeat this until the move ends.

Retracting Fiery Arcs

In the final phase, Hecate releases green flames that retract back to her. Create distance and wait for the flames to return before attacking. Use this time to heal or prepare for your next move.

By understanding these specific moves and employing a strategic approach to each phase of the fight, you can defeat Hecate and continue your journey through the underworld. Remember, each attempt is a learning experience that brings you closer to victory.

CHAPTER 4

Confronting Scylla and the Sirens

Introduction to the Trio

Scylla and the Sirens present one of the more intricate and challenging battles in Hades 2. This formidable trio, each with distinct abilities and attacks, stands as a significant hurdle on Melinoë's journey. The encounter is not just about brute strength; it requires a strategic approach, agility, and keen observation. As you prepare to face Scylla and the Sirens, understanding their unique dynamics and individual threats will be crucial to your success. This guide aims to break down each component of the battle to help you navigate and conquer this daunting trio.

Scylla and the Sirens' Attack List

The battle against Scylla and the Sirens is characterized by a diverse array of attacks. Each member of the trio has a specific set of moves designed to overwhelm and outmaneuver you. Below is a detailed breakdown of their attack patterns and strategies for countering them.

Wailer Attack

Scylla, the most imposing of the trio, initiates the Wailer Attack by shrieking and pursuing you across the arena. This attack is signaled by a high-pitched scream, giving you a brief window to react. To counter this, keep moving and avoid getting cornered. Use your dash ability to create distance and attack her from behind when she pauses.

Four-Beam Attack

Scylla also possesses a Four-Beam Attack, where she emits beams that circle her. These beams can quickly drain your health if you're caught in their path. The key to dodging this attack is to stay outside the beams' range and move in a circular pattern, maintaining a safe distance while looking for opportunities to strike when the beams retract.

Drummer's Red Casts

The Drummer Siren contributes to the chaos with Red Casts that cover portions of the arena. These casts deal significant damage upon contact. They are predictable but deadly, appearing as glowing red zones on the ground. Avoid these areas at all costs and prioritize taking down the Drummer whenever possible to reduce the overall threat level in the arena.

Guitarist's Red Casts and Ring of Power

The Guitarist Siren adds another layer of difficulty with her Red Casts and Ring of Power. The Red Casts function similarly to the Drummer's, but the Ring of Power is particularly dangerous. This move creates a damaging circle that expands from her position. When you see the Guitarist preparing this attack, dash out of the ring's range immediately and use the window when she's casting to deal damage from a safe distance.

Guitarist's Charge Move

The Guitarist also employs a Charge Move, where She dashes across the arena in a straight line. This attack can catch you off guard if you're not paying attention. Watch for her winding up and move perpendicularly to her charge path to avoid getting hit. Use the moments after her charge to counterattack while she recovers.

Bubble Projectile Attack

A more subtle but equally dangerous move is the Bubble Projectile Attack, where the Guitarist shoots bubble-like projectiles at you. These bubbles track your movement and can cause substantial damage. Keep moving to avoid them, and use long-range attacks to interrupt the Guitarist before she releases too many bubbles.

Giant Cast Attacks

The Sirens collectively can unleash Giant Cast Attacks, which force you into specific areas of the arena. One variant forces you near the Drummer, while another pushes you away. These casts are large and hard to dodge if you're not quick. The safest approach is to stay mobile and be prepared to dash out of confined spaces as soon as you see the cast forming.

Weapon Attack

Scylla's Weapon Attack is straightforward but deadly. She swings her weapon when you get too close, causing heavy damage. To counter this, maintain a medium distance from her, striking when she's busy with other attacks, and retreating before she can counter with her weapon.

Spiked Projectile Attack

Lastly, Scylla has a Spiked Projectile Attack, launching a series of spiked projectiles in your direction. These projectiles are relatively slow but cover a wide area. The best strategy is to keep moving laterally and dodge through the gaps between the projectiles. This attack leaves Scylla vulnerable, so take advantage of this opening to deal significant damage.

Strategy to Overcome the Trio

Defeating Scylla and the Sirens requires a tactical approach. Focus on one enemy at a time to reduce the number of active threats. The Drummer is a good initial target due to her stationary nature, followed by the Guitarist, who is more mobile but less dangerous when alone. Save Scylla for last, as her attacks are easier to manage without the distractions from the Sirens.

Always stay on the move to avoid getting trapped by their combined attacks. Use the edges of the arena to your advantage, and don't be afraid to retreat temporarily to regroup and reassess the situation. Prioritize dodging over attacking, especially when multiple attacks are converging on your position.

Understanding each member's actions and skillfully combining your attacks and dodges will allow you to dismantle this fearsome trio and continue your trip farther into the underworld. This encounter requires as much strategic thought and execution as raw skill, making it a memorable and gratifying test in Hades 2.

CHAPTER 5

Battle Strategy for Scylla and the Sirens

Focusing on Individual Band Members

Facing Scylla and the Sirens requires a thoughtful and methodical approach. The trio presents a multi-layered challenge that can be overwhelming if tackled head-on without a plan. The key to success lies in isolating and focusing on one band member at a time. This strategy reduces the overall pressure and chaos of the encounter, allowing you to manage their attacks more effectively.

Scylla: Scylla is the most prominent threat, with her powerful melee attacks and Four-Beam Attack. However, tackling her first might not be the wisest choice due to her durability. Instead, keep an eye on her movements and avoid her swings while you deal with the Sirens.

Drummer Siren: The Drummer is relatively stationary but casts dangerous Red Zones that can control your movement. Start by targeting her. Focus on her casts and ensure you are constantly moving to avoid damaging areas. Eliminating her first significantly reduces the arena's hazards, giving you more freedom to maneuver.

Guitarist Siren: The Guitarist is more mobile and presents a variety of ranged attacks, including Bubble Projectiles and the Ring of Power. After the Drummer is down, shift your focus to the Guitarist. Watch for her Charge Move and maintain distance to avoid her Red Casts. Her mobility can be a challenge, but without the Drummer's pressure, you can better manage her attacks.

By prioritizing the Drummer and then the Guitarist, you'll face less opposition when it's time to take down Scylla. This methodical approach prevents the fight from becoming too overwhelming and allows you to handle each threat in a controlled manner.

Handling Combined Attacks

Scylla and the Sirens are most dangerous when their attacks overlap. This synergy can create chaotic situations where dodging becomes almost impossible. The key to surviving these combined assaults is to maintain situational awareness and adapt your movements to the flow of battle.

Stay Mobile: Constant movement is essential. Never stay in one place for too long, and always be prepared to dash out of danger. The arena will often be covered in hazardous zones and projectiles, so keep an eye on the ground and the positions of each band member.

Use the Arena: Utilize the edges of the arena to your advantage. These areas often provide more room to maneuver and fewer overlapping attack zones. However, be cautious of getting cornered by Scylla's melee attacks.

Watch for Patterns: Each band member has a distinct rhythm to their attacks. Learn these patterns and time your dashes and counters accordingly. For example, after the Guitarist's Charge Move, there's a brief window to land some hits before she recovers.

Prioritize Defense: It can be tempting to go all out with attacks, but in this battle, survival comes first. Focus on dodging and avoiding damage more than dealing with it. Look for safe opportunities to strike rather than forcing an opening.

By keeping these strategies in mind, you can better manage the combined attacks and avoid getting overwhelmed. Patience and precision are crucial to emerging victorious in this chaotic encounter.

Key Survival Tips

Success in the battle against Scylla and the Sirens hinges on a few key survival strategies. These tips can help you stay alive and maintain the upper hand throughout the fight.

Keep Moving: Never stay still. Constant movement helps avoid many of the area attacks and keeps you unpredictable. Use your dash to quickly reposition and evade.

Manage Resources: Pay attention to your health and abilities. Use healing items and power-ups strategically to ensure you're in the best possible shape for the fight. Don't hesitate to use a powerful ability if it can turn the tide in your favor.

Focus Fire: Concentrate your attacks on one band member at a time. This focused approach helps you eliminate threats more efficiently and reduces the number of simultaneous attacks you have to deal with.

Learn from Defeats: If you don't succeed initially, take note of what went wrong. Understanding the timing and patterns of the trio's attacks can significantly improve your chances in subsequent attempts.

Stay Calm: It's easy to get flustered when under constant assault. Keep a cool head and remember that every attack has a counter. Panicking will only lead to mistakes and missed opportunities.

These survival tips are designed to keep you on your toes and maximize your effectiveness in battle. With practice, you'll find yourself navigating the fight with greater confidence and precision.

Rewards for Defeating Scylla and the Sirens

Conquering Scylla and the Sirens is no small feat, and the rewards for doing so are well worth the effort. Successfully defeating this trio not only progresses the storyline but also provides valuable items and upgrades.

Unique Loot: Upon victory, you'll receive unique items specific to this encounter. These items often include powerful weapons or enhancements that can give you an edge in future battles.

Experience Points: Defeating such a formidable challenge grants a significant amount of experience points. This boost can help you level up faster, unlocking new abilities and improving your overall power.

Story Progression: Overcoming Scylla and the Sirens often unlocks new areas or story elements. This progression is crucial for advancing in the game and uncovering more of the rich narrative.

Bragging Rights: Lastly, defeating this challenging trio is a testament to your skill and strategy. It's a memorable achievement that you can take pride in and share with fellow players.

The rewards for this battle are designed to enhance your gameplay experience and provide a satisfying sense of accomplishment. By mastering the strategies and tips outlined, you'll not only conquer Scylla and the Sirens but also reap the benefits of your hard-fought victory.

CHAPTER 6

Battling Eris: Guardian of the Rift

Introduction to Eris

Eris, the Guardian of the Rift, is a formidable adversary known for her chaotic and unpredictable battle style. As a key figure in the world of Hades 2, Eris combines agility, devastating attacks, and strategic summoning abilities, making her a tough challenge for any player. Confronting Eris requires not just strength but also a keen understanding of her patterns and tactics. This guide will go over the subtleties of fighting Eris, including extensive knowledge into her move list and techniques for overcoming her powerful defenses.

Eris's Move List and Descriptions

Bomb Throws

One of Eris's primary attacks involves hurling explosive bombs across the arena. These bombs have a short fuse and explode upon impact, dealing significant damage within a certain radius. The key to avoiding these bombs is to stay on the move. Eris tends to throw them in quick succession, creating a series of explosive zones. Pay attention to her animation cues—she'll wind up slightly before each throw, giving you a moment to dash out of the way. The blast radius can catch you off guard, so always aim to move in a zigzag pattern rather than a straight line.

Projectile Spins

In this move, Eris unleashes a flurry of spinning projectiles that radiate outwards in a circular pattern. These projectiles travel quickly and can cover a large area, making them particularly dangerous in close quarters. When you see Eris preparing for a spin, it's best to create distance between you and her. Use the outer edges of the arena to your advantage and dodge between the gaps in the projectiles. Timing is crucial here; wait for the projectiles to begin spreading before making your move to avoid getting hit.

Enemy Summons

Eris can summon additional enemies to the battlefield, adding another layer of complexity to the fight. These minions vary in type and attack style, from melee attackers to ranged casters. It's essential to deal with these summons promptly. Focus on eliminating them quickly to prevent being overwhelmed. Use area-of-effect attacks if you have them to clear groups of enemies efficiently. Keeping the number of summons to a minimum allows you to concentrate more on Eris and her direct attacks.

V-Shaped Projectile Waves

One of Eris's signature moves is the V-shaped projectile wave. She launches a series of projectiles that spread out in a V-formation, covering a wide area. This attack can be tricky to dodge due to its spread and speed. The best strategy is to observe the gaps between the projectiles and position yourself accordingly. Move to the side of the V formation to find safer spots. Practice makes perfect with this move; learning the timing and patterns will significantly reduce the damage you take.

Arena Marking Bombs

Eris employs a more deliberate attack, throwing bombs that mark certain locations in the arena. After a brief interval, these marked patches explode, causing damage to everyone in the vicinity. The objective is to maintain track of these indicated zones while avoiding Eris' other attacks. When you see her throw these bombs, take note of their places and move away. To avoid being caught in the delayed explosions, you must keep mobile and aware of your surroundings at all times.

Targeting Laser

Eris's targeting laser is one of her most dangerous moves. She focuses a laser on a specific player, locking on before firing a devastating beam. This attack requires quick reflexes and constant movement. As soon as you see the targeting laser appear, start moving in unpredictable patterns. Dash frequently to break the laser's lock-on and avoid the beam. The key here is not to stay in one place for too long, as the laser adjusts to your position rapidly.

Strategies for Battling Eris

General Strategy

Facing Eris demands a balanced approach that combines offense and defense. Start by familiarizing yourself with her attack patterns. Each move has distinct visual and auditory cues that can help you anticipate her next action. Stay patient and avoid reckless attacks. Focus on dodging and counter-attacking during windows of opportunity.

Phase Breakdown

Eris's battle can be divided into distinct phases, each with escalating difficulty. Initially, she may rely more on Bomb Throws and Projectile Spins. As the fight progresses, expect an increase in the frequency and intensity of her more complex moves like Enemy Summons and the Targeting Laser. Adapt your strategy as the phases change. In the early phase, prioritize learning her patterns. In later stages, focus on endurance and precision to avoid her high-damage attacks.

Handling Specific Moves

Bomb Throws: Stay mobile and watch for the wind-up animation to dodge effectively.

Projectile Spins: Keep distance and utilize the arena's outer edges to maneuver through gaps.

Enemy Summons: Quickly eliminate minions to prevent being overwhelmed.

V-Shaped Projectile Waves: Position yourself at the sides of the formation to find safe zones.

Arena Marking Bombs: Be vigilant of marked spots and maintain awareness of your surroundings.

Targeting Laser: Move unpredictably and dash frequently to break the laser's lock.

CHAPTER 7

Strategy to Defeat Eris

Eris, the Guardian of the Rift, is a challenging foe whose chaotic attacks and strategic summons can easily overwhelm unprepared players. Conquering her requires a well-thought-out strategy, a carefully chosen loadout, and an understanding of how to use the environment to your advantage. The following steps will take you through the best ways to beat Eris, including the optimal loadout, weapon options, boons, hexes, and battle strategies.

Best Load out Against Eris

Before engaging Eris, it's crucial to equip yourself with the best possible gear. A balanced loadout should prioritize both offense and defense, allowing you to deal significant damage while surviving her relentless attacks.

Primary Weapon: Choose a weapon that complements your playstyle and allows for quick movements and versatile attacks.

Secondary Weapon: Equip a secondary weapon that provides ranged capabilities or crowd control to manage Eris's summons effectively.

Armor and Accessories: Opt for gear that boosts your health, reduces incoming damage, and enhances your mobility. Items that offer bonuses against boss enemies or improve your resistance to elemental damage can be particularly useful.

Best Weapon Choices

Selecting the right weapon can make a significant difference in your battle against Eris. Here are some top recommendations:

Sword of Shadows: This weapon offers a balanced mix of speed and power, making it ideal for both offense and defense. Its quick attacks can keep Eris on her toes, while its special abilities can deal with her summons effectively.

Bow of Artemis: If you prefer a ranged approach, the Bow of Artemis provides excellent distance attacks and precision. It allows you to stay mobile and keep a safe distance from Eris's more dangerous moves.

Spear of Hades: The spear's reach and versatility make it a solid choice. Its ability to attack from mid-range and control space can help manage Eris's aggressive tactics.

Shield of Aegis: For players who prefer a defensive style, the Shield of Aegis offers robust protection and counter-attack capabilities. Its blocking feature can mitigate damage from Eris's explosive and projectile attacks.

Recommended Boons and Hexes

Boons and hexes can significantly enhance your Abilities and give you an edge in the fight against Eris. Here are some of the best options:

Athena's Boon (Divine Strike): Adds deflection to your attacks, allowing you to reflect Eris's projectiles and reduce incoming damage.

Zeus's Boon (Thunder Dash): Grants lightning damage to your dash, providing additional damage while you maneuver around Eris.

Aphrodite's Boon (Heartbreak Strike): Increases your attack power and applies a weakening effect, reducing Eris's damage output.

Hex of Frailty: Reduces the damage of all enemies, including Eris, making it easier to withstand her onslaught.

Hex of Binding: Temporarily immobilizes summoned enemies, giving you breathing room to focus on Eris herself.

Effective Combat Techniques

Mastering combat techniques is crucial to overcoming Eris's diverse and dangerous move set. Here are some key strategies:

Dodge and Weave: Constant movement is essential. Eris's attacks often cover large areas, so staying mobile and unpredictable will help you avoid damage.

Focus Fire: Target Eris directly whenever possible, but don't neglect her summons. Clearing the battlefield of minions quickly will prevent you from getting overwhelmed.

Timing and Precision: Learn the cues for Eris's attacks. Each move has a specific wind-up, giving you a brief window to react. Time your dodges and attacks to exploit these moments.

Use Special Attacks Wisely: Your weapon's special abilities can turn the tide of battle. Use them strategically to deal with multiple enemies or to interrupt Eris's more powerful moves.

Using the Environment to Your Advantage

The battlefield itself can be a valuable ally if used correctly. Here are some tips for leveraging the environment against Eris:

Pillars and Obstacles: Use pillars and other obstacles to break the line of sight and avoid direct hits from Eris's targeting laser and projectile attacks. These structures can also provide brief respite during more intense phases of the fight.

Arena Boundaries: Position yourself near the edges of the arena to better manage Eris's V-shaped projectile waves and spinning attacks. The boundaries can help you gauge safe zones and reduce the effective area of her attacks.

Elevations and Platforms: If the arena features varying elevations, use them to your advantage. Higher ground can give you a strategic vantage point for ranged attacks, while lower areas can provide cover from certain moves.

CHAPTER 8

Advanced Combat Tactics

In Hades 2's grueling confrontations, learning advanced combat strategies can make the difference between victory and defeat. By improving your talents and learning the specifics of fighting, you can become a strong enemy capable of defeating even the most powerful opponents. In this section, we'll look at three main ways for improving your combat abilities: increasing damage output, perfecting dodge and dash skills, and exploiting boss weaknesses.

Maximizing Damage Output

Dealing with damage efficiently is essential in Hades 2, where every strike counts against powerful adversaries. Here are some tips for maximizing your damage output:

Combo Attacks: Learn to chain together light and heavy attacks to create devastating combos. Experiment with different weapon combinations to discover synergies that amplify your damage potential.

Critical Hits: Take advantage of opportunities to land critical hits, which deal significantly more damage than regular attacks. Look for boons and abilities that increase your critical hit chance, and aim for vulnerable spots on enemies to maximize your damage.

Status Effects: Use status effects to your advantage by applying debuffs to enemies or exploiting their weaknesses. Abilities that inflict poison, burn, or freeze can chip away at enemy health over time, while also providing additional crowd control.

Weapon Enhancements: Upgrade your weapons with enchantments and enhancements to boost their damage output. Experiment with different weapon mods and abilities to find the combination that best suits your playstyle and maximizes your damage potential.

Mastering Dodge and Dash

Survival in Hades 2 often hinges on your ability to dodge and dash with precision and timing. Here's how to master these essential movement techniques:

Evasive Maneuvers: Practice dodging and dashing to avoid enemy attacks while maintaining your position in combat. Learn the timing and range of enemy attacks to anticipate their movements and evade them effectively.

Directional Dodging: Experiment with dodging in different directions to throw off your opponent's aim and create openings for counterattacks. Mastering directional dodging allows you to evade incoming attacks while positioning yourself for a strategic advantage.

Dash Combos: Combine dodging and dashing with attacks to execute fluid and dynamic combat sequences. Use dashes to close the distance between you and your opponent, then follow up with quick strikes to exploit openings in their defenses.

Environmental Awareness: Pay attention to your surroundings and use environmental obstacles to your advantage. Dash behind the cover to avoid incoming projectiles or leap over obstacles to gain high ground and surprise your enemies from above.

Exploiting Boss Weaknesses

Every boss in Hades 2 has its own unique set of strengths and weaknesses, and exploiting these vulnerabilities is key to emerging victorious. Here are some strategies for identifying and capitalizing on boss weaknesses:

Observation: Study each boss's attack patterns and behaviors to identify potential weaknesses or vulnerabilities. Look for openings in their defenses or moments of vulnerability that you can exploit to deal extra damage.

Elemental Weaknesses: Many bosses in Hades 2 have specific elemental weaknesses that you can exploit to your advantage. Use weapons or abilities that deal elemental damage corresponding to the boss's weakness to maximize your damage output.

Staggering Attacks: Some bosses are susceptible to staggering or interrupting attacks that temporarily immobilize or incapacitate them. Look for opportunities to stagger bosses by targeting their weak points or using abilities that inflict stagger effects.

Strategic Positioning: Position yourself strategically during boss battles to maximize your damage output while minimizing your exposure to danger. Stay mobile and agile, and use cover or environmental obstacles to protect yourself from incoming attacks.

By mastering these advanced combat tactics, you'll be well-equipped to face the challenges that await you in Hades 2. Experiment with different strategies, adapt to the strengths and weaknesses of each opponent and never stop honing your skills. With perseverance and determination, you'll become a true master of combat in the underworld.

CHAPTER 9

Exploring Further Challenges

After learning the main activities and overcoming the first obstacles of Hades 2, you may wonder what lies ahead. The game includes a multitude of additional content and challenges that will put your abilities, strategy, and perseverance to the test. In this phase, we'll look at the additional content available in Hades 2 and offer crucial recommendations for success in the endgame.

Additional Content in Hades 2

The world of Hades 2 is rich with extra content that goes beyond the main storyline. These challenges and features are designed to provide hours of additional gameplay, keeping you engaged and continuously testing your abilities. Here's an overview of what you can expect:

Elysium Trials: Once you've beaten the primary campaign, the Elysium Trials offer a series of increasingly difficult encounters. These trials are meant to push your combat skills to the limit, with tougher enemies, more complex mechanics, and fewer resources. Each trial level provides unique rewards that can enhance your abilities or provide rare items.

Hidden Bosses: As you progress through the game, you will encounter hidden bosses that demand unique techniques to overcome. These fights are frequently more difficult than the major plot bosses, including sophisticated attack patterns and larger damage outputs. Defeating secret bosses can result in large prizes and unlock extraordinary powers.

Ascension Mode: For those seeking the ultimate test of skill, Ascension Mode allows you to replay the game with added difficulty modifiers. These modifiers can include stronger enemies, reduced health, limited resources, and more. Each level of Ascension Mode increases the challenge, offering greater rewards and achievements.

Lore Expansions: Go closer into Hades 2's complex tale by discovering additional lore via side missions and secret treasures. Interact with NPCs, explore old artifacts, and access hidden dialogues to learn more about the game's setting, characters, and history.

Custom Challenges: Create your custom challenges by adjusting game parameters such as enemy strength, health regeneration, and item availability. Share your custom challenges with the community and try to complete challenges created by other players for endless gameplay possibilities.

Tips for Endgame Success

Precisely the way you progress through Hades 2's endgame content, the stakes increase and the difficulties get more difficult. Here are some crucial ideas to help you succeed:

Optimize Your Build: In the endgame, every stat and ability counts. Focus on optimizing your build to suit your playstyle. Prioritize abilities that synergize well with your preferred weapons and combat strategies. Experiment with different combinations to find the most effective setup for the challenges ahead.

Resource Management: Efficiently managing your resources is crucial in the endgame. Ensure you have a balanced supply of health potions, mana regenerators, and other consumables. Plan your resource usage strategically to avoid running out during critical moments.

Study Enemy Patterns: Each endgame enemy and boss has distinct attack patterns and behaviors. Take the time to study these patterns and learn their tells. Understanding when to dodge, block, or counterattack can significantly increase your chances of survival.

Adaptability: Be prepared to adapt your strategies based on the situation. The endgame often requires quick thinking and flexibility. If a particular tactic isn't working, don't hesitate to switch up your approach and try new techniques.

Utilize Environment: The endgame levels are often designed with environmental elements that can be used to your advantage. Look for cover, traps, and high ground to gain a strategic edge over your enemies. Using the environment effectively can turn the tide of battle in your favor.

Level Up Strategically: Focus on leveling up abilities and stats that provide the most benefit for endgame content. Prioritize health, damage output, and defensive abilities. Make sure to enhance skills that complement your playstyle and the specific challenges you're facing.

Gear Up: Equip the best gear available to you. Look for equipment with high stats and beneficial effects. Don't hesitate to invest in upgrading your gear to maximize its potential. Legendary and rare items can provide significant boosts to your capabilities.

Master Your Combos: In the endgame, precision and timing are everything. Practice and perfect your attack combos to maximize damage while minimizing exposure to enemy attacks. Chain your abilities and attacks smoothly to keep the pressure on your opponents.

Community Strategies: Engage with the Hades 2 community to learn from others' experiences. Share tips, strategies, and builds with fellow players. Participating in community discussions can provide new insights and help you overcome particularly challenging content.

Patience and Perseverance: Endgame content is designed to be challenging, so patience and perseverance are key. Don't get discouraged by repeated failures. Learn from each attempt and gradually improve your strategies and skills.

By exploring the additional content and applying these tips for endgame success, you can continue to enjoy the rich and challenging world of Hades 2 long after completing the main storyline. The game's depth and complexity offer endless opportunities for growth and mastery, ensuring a rewarding experience for dedicated players.

CONCLUSION

Once you near the end of this book, it's time to consider the methods, skills, and insights you've gained while preparing for your travels in Hades 2. This part will summarize the important strategies we've addressed, lay out the path for continuing your adventure, and thank the designers and collaborators who made this guide possible.

Recap of Key Strategies

Throughout this guide, we've covered essential tactics and strategies designed to help you excel in Hades 2. Let's revisit some of the most crucial points:

Understanding Boss Mechanics: Knowing your enemies is half the battle. Each boss in Hades 2 has unique attack patterns and behaviors. By studying these, you can anticipate their moves, dodge effectively, and strike at the right moment.

Preparation for Battles: Equip yourself wisely. Choose weapons and gear that suit your playstyle and enhance your strengths. Don't forget to stock up on essential items such as health potions and mana regenerators.

Maximizing Damage Output: Optimize your build by focusing on abilities and equipment that increase your damage. Learn and master attack combos to inflict maximum damage on your foes.

Mastering Dodge and Dash: These maneuvers are your best defense. Practice dodging and dashing to avoid attacks and reposition yourself strategically during combat.

Exploiting Boss Weaknesses: Each boss has specific weaknesses. Use the right weapons and abilities to exploit these vulnerabilities and bring them down more efficiently.

Resource Management: Efficiently manage your resources throughout your journey. Use your items strategically and ensure you have a balanced supply to sustain you through prolonged battles.

Utilizing the Environment: The battlefield is more than just a backdrop. Use environmental elements to your advantage, whether it's taking cover, using traps, or gaining higher ground.

Adapting Strategies: Be flexible in your approach. If one strategy isn't working, be prepared to switch tactics and try different methods to overcome the challenges you face.

Community Engagement: Don't hesitate to tap into the collective knowledge of the Hades 2 community. Sharing tips, builds, and experiences with fellow players can provide new perspectives and strategies.

Continuing Your Journey

Your journey in Hades 2 doesn't end with the completion of the main storyline. The game offers a vast array of additional content and challenges to keep you engaged:

Elysium Trials: Test your skills in these increasingly difficult encounters. The Elysium Trials are designed to push you to your limits and offer unique rewards for those who succeed.

Hidden Bosses: Seek out and conquer hidden bosses. These formidable opponents require advanced strategies and offer significant rewards upon defeat.

Ascension Mode: For the ultimate challenge, try Ascension Mode. With added difficulty modifiers, this mode will truly test your mastery of the game's mechanics and your ability to adapt under pressure.

Lore Exploration: plunge further into the rich lore of Hades 2. Complete side quests, interact with

NPCs and uncover hidden stories to gain a deeper understanding of the game's world and characters.

Custom Challenges: Create and share custom challenges with the community. Experiment with different parameters to keep the gameplay fresh and exciting.

Community Events: Participate in community events and challenges. Engaging with the Hades 2 community can provide new opportunities for collaboration and competition.

Personal Goals: Set your own goals and milestones. Whether it's mastering a particular weapon, achieving a flawless boss run, or collecting all rare items, personal objectives can add new layers of satisfaction to your journey.

Acknowledgments and Credits

This guide wouldn't have been possible without the efforts and contributions of many individuals and resources:

Developers of Hades 2: Thank you for creating such a rich and immersive game that has captivated the hearts of many players. Your creativity and hard work have provided countless hours of enjoyment and challenge.

Community Contributors: A special thank you to the Hades 2 community. Your shared strategies, tips, and insights have been invaluable in compiling this guide. The community's passion and dedication have made this game even more enjoyable.

Guide Contributors: To everyone who has provided feedback, shared their experiences and contributed to the development of this guide, your input has been essential. Your knowledge and expertise have helped create a comprehensive and useful resource for players.

Readers and Players: Finally, thank you to the readers and players who have used this guide. Your enthusiasm for Hades 2 and your pursuit of excellence in the game inspires us to continue creating content that enhances your gaming experience.

As you continue your adventure in Hades 2, remember that each challenge is an opportunity to grow and improve. The strategies and insights provided in this guide are tools to help you achieve success, but the true essence of the game lies in your perseverance, adaptability, and enjoyment. Good luck, and may your adventures in the Underworld be filled with triumph and discovery.

www.ingramcontent.com/pod-product-compliance
Lightning Source LLC
Chambersburg PA
CBHW050235230526
45470CB00005B/1969